WHY MARTÍN DE LEÓN MATTERS TO TEXAS

By Lynn Peppas

Published in 2014 by The Rosen Publishing Group, Inc.
29 East 21st Street, New York, NY 10010

Copyright © 2014 by Digital Discovery Publishing

All rights reserved. No part of this book may be reproduced in any form without permission in writing from the publisher, except by a reviewer.

First Edition

Developed, written, and produced by Digital Discovery Publishing
Editors: Molly Aloian, Wendy Scavuzzo
Design & Production: Katherine Berti
Curriculum & content coordinator: Reagan Miller
Photo research: Crystal Sikkens, Allison Napier
Proofreader: Sarah Cairns

Photo Credits: Amon Carter Museum: 24 (top)
Corbis: 19
De Agostini Picture Library / G. Dagli Orti / The Bridgeman Art Library: 23 (top)
Dolph Briscoe Center for American History, Austin, Texas: 21
The Granger Collection, NYC: 16 (top), 28
Courtesy of LaRue Roth, Victoria CVB: 25 (bottom), 30
Library of Congress: 9 (bottom), 7 (bottom), 13
National Library of Medicine: 29
North Wind Picture Archives: 7 (top), 10 (left), 11 (top), 14, 15 (top), 16 (bottom), 20, 27
Rugeley-Moore Collection, Richmond, Texas: 8
Shutterstock: 3, 5, 6, 15
Wikimedia Commons: cover, 10 (top), 11 (bottom), 12, 17

Maps by Digital Discovery Publishing: pages 5, 6

All websites were live and accurate at the time of printing.

Library of Congress Cataloging-in-Publication Data

Peppas, Lynn.
Why Martin de Leon matters to Texas / by Lynn Peppas.
 p. cm. – (Texas perspectives)
Includes index.
ISBN 978-1-4777-0916-0 (library binding) – ISBN 978-1-4777-0941-2 (pbk.) – ISBN 978-1-4777-0942-9 (6-pack)
1. Leon, Martin de, 1765-1833 – Juvenile literature. 2. Pioneers – Texas – Victoria – Biography – Juvenile literature. 3. Victoria (Tex.) – History – Juvenile literature. I. Peppas, Lynn. II. Title.
F394.V6 P47 2013
976.4–dc23

Manufactured in the United States of America

CPSIA Compliance Information: Batch W13PK: For Further Information contact Rosen Publishing, New York, New York at 1-800-237-9932

CONTENTS

Chapter 1 . . . . . **Texas Dreams** 4

Chapter 2 . . . . . **Early Life** 6

Chapter 3 . . . . . **Moving to Texas** 12

Chapter 4 . . . . . **A New Colony** 18

Chapter 5 . . . . . **Victoria** 22

Chapter 6 . . . . . **De León Ranch** 26

Chapter 7 . . . . . **Legacy** 29

Learning More 30

Timeline 31

Glossary 32

Index 32

1 TEXAS DREAMS

Martín De León was just a teenager when he fearlessly began leading his mule train from Mexico to Texas. Martín brought much-needed goods, on the backs of mules, to miners in the Mexican state of Texas. It was a very dangerous job. Indian tribes hid in the nearby mountains and attacked and stole from passing mule trains. Luckily, Martín knew how to fight off Indian attacks.

DREAMING OF A COLONY

Martín enjoyed the adventure so much that he joined the Mexican military in 1785, when he was 20 years old. There he earned the reputation of being a brave soldier as he fought Indians. He was even made a captain, which was the highest rank he could achieve. Martín also loved the wild, untamed lands of Texas. He dreamed of one day starting his own **colony** there.

It would take almost 40 years, but Martín did make his dream come true. In 1824, he became the first Mexican empresario to begin a colony in Texas.

From a letter to Martín on April 13, 1824:

> [H]aving duly considered the petition of Martin De León...[requesting] permission to... [settle] on the banks of the river Guadalupe, with the intention of founding and building up a town, [we] have resolved to admit the petition.

During his lifetime, Martín became well known for his bravery, his **hospitality**, and his love and respect for his family and religion. He was also a successful businessman and one of the first cattle ranchers in Texas.

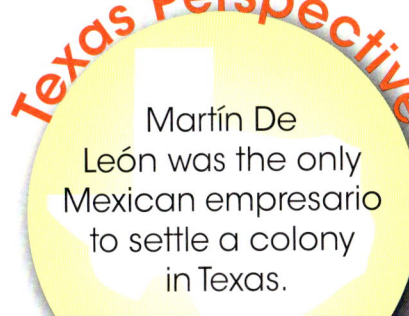

Texas Perspective

Martín De León was the only Mexican empresario to settle a colony in Texas.

MARTÍN DE LEÓN'S TEXAS

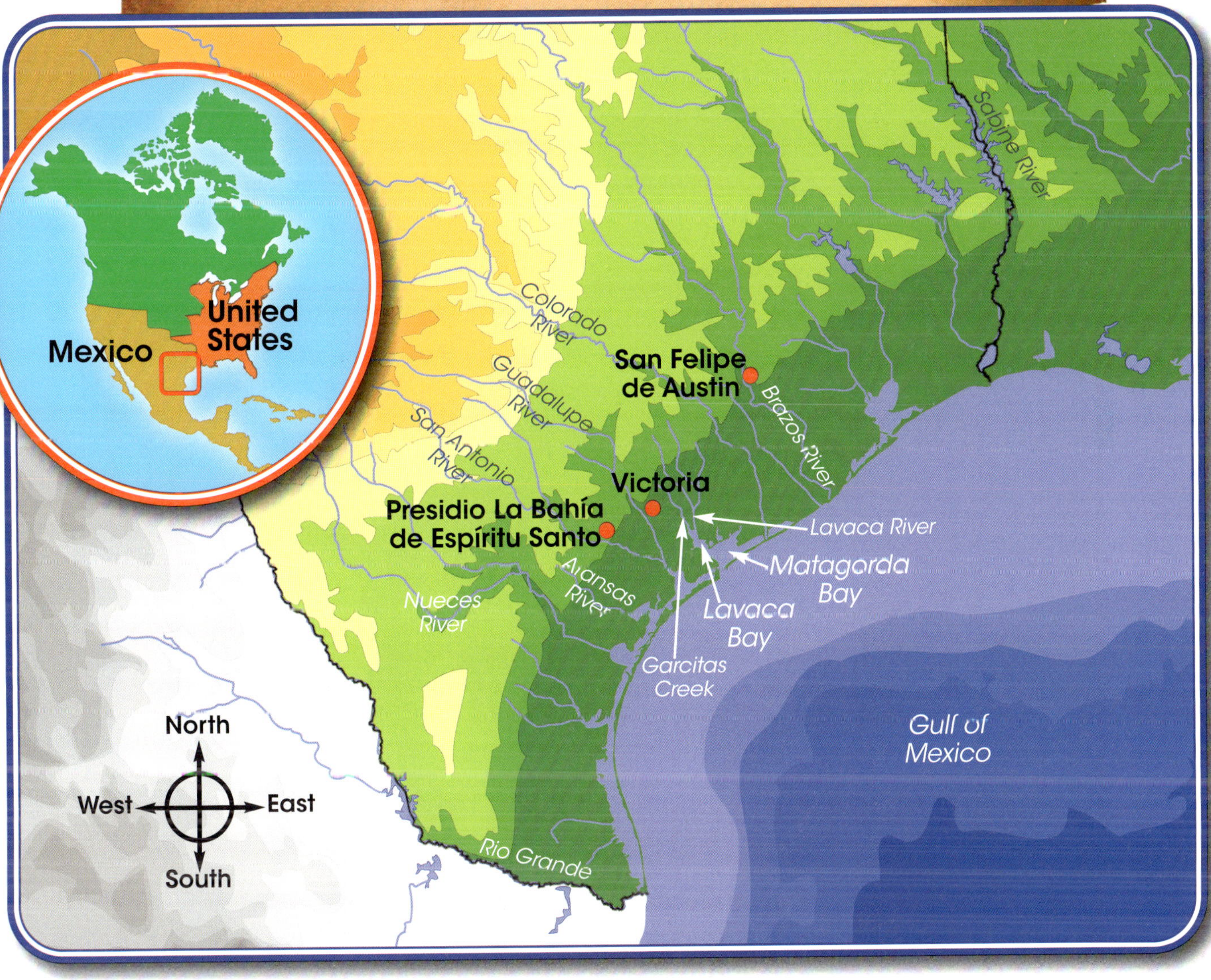

2 EARLY LIFE

Martín De León was born in Burgos, Mexico, in 1765. Burgos is a town in the Mexican **province** of Nuevo Santander. Martín's father, Bernardo, came from a wealthy family of Spanish **nobles**. Many of Martín's **ancestors** were in the military or were statesmen. Bernardo traveled with his family from Spain to Mexico. They settled in Nuevo Santander in 1748.

GROWING UP

Martín grew up in a nearby mining town called Cruillas. He learned to ride horses on his family's ranch and was a skilled horseman. There were no public schools in the area at the time, so Martín's father paid a local **friar** to teach Martín and his brothers. Later, Martín's parents wanted him to go to Spain to study and become a statesman. Martín had different ideas for his future, though. He wanted to stay in New Spain and join the military instead.

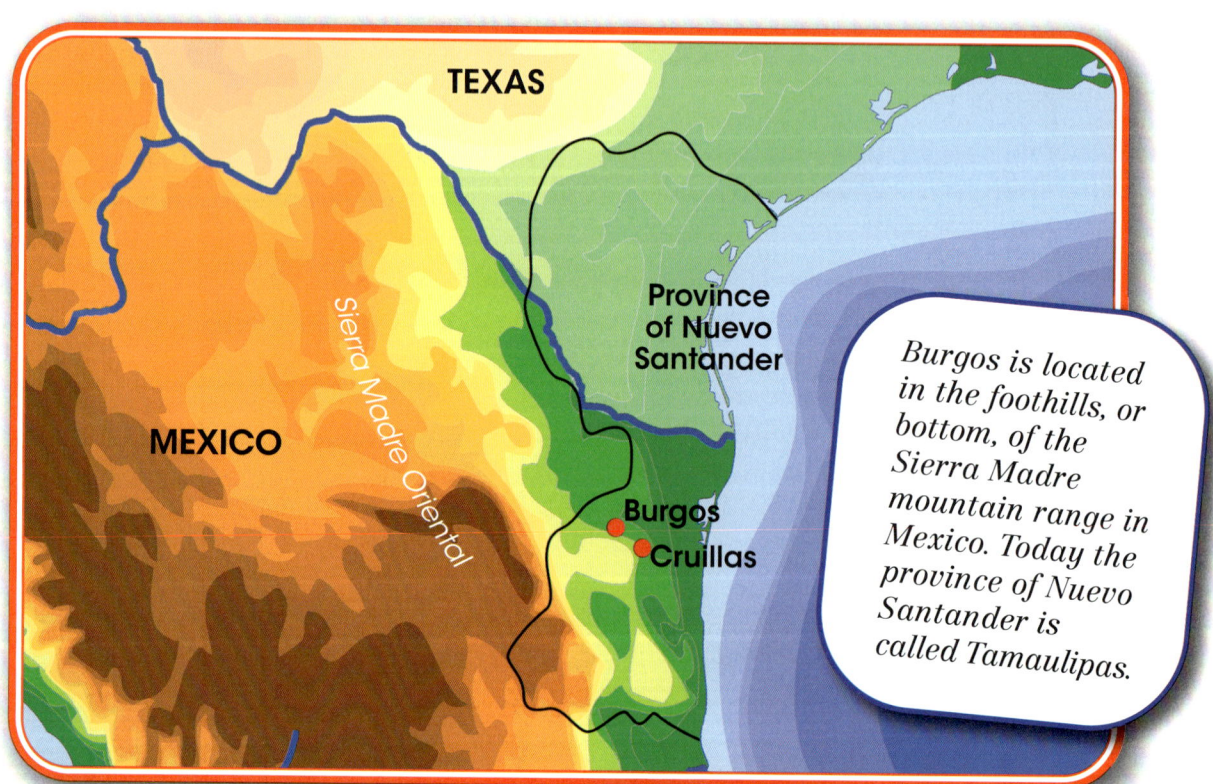

Burgos is located in the foothills, or bottom, of the Sierra Madre mountain range in Mexico. Today the province of Nuevo Santander is called Tamaulipas.

6

Spanish soldiers roamed the Mexican countryside. They captured Indians and forced them to be slaves.

INDIAN RELATIONS

From the 1500s to the 1800s, much of Mexico and all of Texas were unsettled areas. Indians had lived in these areas for thousands of years before Spanish explorers arrived. Some Indians got along with the Spanish and even traded goods with them. Others did not like the Spanish because they took over their lands and forced them into slavery. Some tribes fought back by raiding Spanish settlements, such as those in the Mexican province of Nuevo Santander.

NEW SPAIN

The Spanish first arrived in the area we know as Mexico in the early 1500s. They called it the "New World" because it was a newly discovered area. They claimed the area for Spain. From 1519 to 1821, Mexico was part of New Spain. New Spain was ruled by Spanish governors called viceroys. A viceroy is a person who represents the king in a faraway colony.

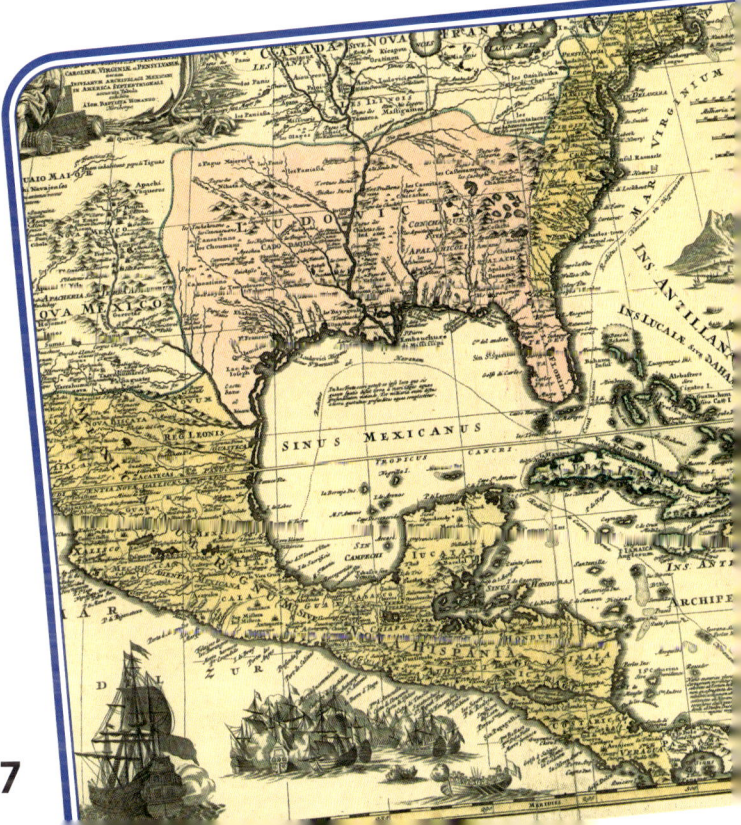

Around the time of Martín's birth, New Spain included Mexico and stretched across the southern part of what is now the United States.

A mule is a cross between a male donkey and a female horse.

MULE TRAIN

The 18-year-old Martín De León's first job was as a head muleteer. A muleteer is a person who uses mule trains to move goods and supplies to others who need them. Martín moved his goods by mule train and hired workers to help him.

Nuevo Santander had mining towns that traded goods such as salt, silver, copper, gold, and lead. Martín brought these goods from Nuevo Santander to Mexico City, where he picked up and brought back food and supplies. It was a dangerous job because the mule teams traveled over unguarded lands. The men fought off hungry animals, Indians, or thieves they met along the way.

A passage from the book *De León: A Tejano Family History* describes how muleteers dressed:

> *They used a felt or straw hat with a wide brim and a low crown decorated with silver ornaments in various shapes (stars, heads of eagles, of bulls, etc.)…their jacket was short and made of wool or suede…they wore manly felt or suede trousers which buttoned up the side, and their boots, which reached above the calf…were made of two thick deer skins…*

FIGHTING INDIANS

In 1790, Martín joined a military **regiment** called the Fieles de Burgos. In English the name means "people faithful to Burgos." It was the regiment's job to protect settlers from Indian attacks in Nuevo Santander. Martín was a good soldier and was **promoted** to captain. It was the highest rank a Mexican-born officer could hold.

SECOND-CLASS CITIZENS

In New Spain in the 1700s, people who were born in Spain had more rights than people born in Mexico. People born in Spain were called peninsulars. They were first-class **citizens**. People who were born in Mexico but had Spanish ancestors were called criollos. They were considered second-class citizens. The term "second-class citizen" describes a person who is thought less of than a first-class citizen. Martín De León was a criollo.

▲ *Mexican viceroy Juan Vicente de Güemes organized the Fieles de Burgos regiment to protect Nuevo Santander against Indian attacks.*

Mestizos, or people of mixed Spanish and Indian heritage, had even fewer rights than criollos.

CHILDHOOD STORIES

Bernardo De León told his sons exciting and true stories of Spanish explorers who had come to New Spain 100 years before. A favorite was the story of a Spanish explorer named Alonso De León. This De León, who shared the same name but was not related, searched the coast of Texas for the French explorer Sieur de La Salle and his colony, called Fort St. Louis.

Sieur de La Salle was a French explorer who founded a colony in Texas in 1687. The French colony was seen as a threat to the Spanish living in Mexico.

STARTING A FAMILY

Martín met and fell in love with a young woman named Patricia de la Garza. She lived in the port city of Soto la Marina and was the daughter of De León's military commander. They married in 1795. Patricia came from a wealthy family who gave Martín a **dowry**, or gifts, when he married their daughter. Patricia's dowry included a large amount of money, horses, donkeys, and cows.

For the next five years, the couple lived in Burgos where Martín kept working as a soldier. They also ran a ranch. They soon became parents and, over the next 20 years, the De León family grew to include ten children. The couple had four boys, named Fernando, Silvestre, Felix, and Agapito. They had six girls, named Candelaria, Guadalupe, Maria Jesusa, Refugia, Augustina, and Francisca.

LOUISIANA PURCHASE

The French explorer Sieur de La Salle claimed a large area of land in North America in the name of France in 1682. He called it Louisiana to honor King Louis XIV. Today, this area is made up of Louisiana, Mississippi, and parts of Texas and Alabama. Spain owned the land that surrounded Louisiana, such as the rest of Texas and Florida.

In 1803, France sold Louisiana to the United States in a **treaty** agreement called the Louisiana Purchase. Spain and the United States argued over who owned land in Texas.

SPANISH MISSIONS

Spanish leaders decided to start colonies in Texas to protect it from the French. Spanish friars and soldiers settled small communities, called missions, throughout Texas to protect the land. Indians from different tribes lived at the missions. Friars taught the Indians their Spanish traditions and **converted** them to **Christianity**.

Mission Nuestra Señora de la Purísima Concepción de Acuña was founded in 1716. It was built to protect Spanish territory from the French in Louisiana. The mission was moved near the San Antonio River in 1731.

3 MOVING TO TEXAS

Martín first came to Texas as the captain of his military regiment. He liked what he saw and decided that it would be a good place to settle a new ranch. In early 1801, he moved his wife and young family to La Bahía del Espíritu Santo on the San Antonio River in Texas.

RANCHO SANTA MARGARITA

The De Leóns settled on the Nueces River and built a ranch they called Santa Margarita. Their ranch was far away from the safety of the presidio on the San Antonio River. A small group of workers lived on the De León ranch, too. Cowhands, called *vaqueros* in Spanish, helped with the cattle and horses. Farmworkers, called *peones*, planted and harvested fruits and vegetables such as corn, tomatoes, beans, and squash. The wives of the peones and vaqueros helped with the household chores such as cooking, cleaning, and caring for the men and children.

PRESIDIOS IN TEXAS

Presidio is the Spanish name for a fort protected by Spanish soldiers. New settlers to the area built their homes and ranches close to the presidio so they would be protected.

Presidios had turrets along the walls (right) to defend against attacks. Large gates (left) also protected settlers inside.

12

COLONY DENIED

Martín **petitioned** the Spanish governor to start a colony. A petition is a formal document that asks for something from the government. The Spanish government denied Martín's petition and did not allow him to begin a colony. Martín tried again in 1809, but the government denied his petition again.

NEW HOMES IN TEXAS

La Bahía del Espíritu Santo was located in the flat plains area of Texas. There were no tall trees around from which to make homes. Most settlers built homes called *jacales*. Posts were set in the ground and walls were made from the branches of shrubs or small trees. These branches were laid on the ground and stacked flat on top of each other. A mixture of mud and straw was used as a plaster to fill in any openings. There were no windows, but opening slits were made with just enough room for a gun to poke through. This was so those living in the homes could shoot at Indians or other attackers.

The jacales in this drawing are similar to ones built in Texas where Martín De León settled.

A NEW LIFE

Martín made his living as a horseman, called a *caballero* in Spanish. He and the vaqueros on his ranch caught and tamed wild mustangs to sell. Martín and other ranchers rounded up herds of wild horses by chasing them on horseback. The vaqueros then herded the horses into fenced areas. Martín sold horses and mules to other ranchers or soldiers who needed them.

Texas Perspective

Martín De León is known as one of the first trail drivers in Texas.

TRAIL DRIVING

Martín and his vaqueros also rode horses to round up wild cattle in the spring and fall of every year. They collected a herd and drove it back to the ranch. Martín and his vaqueros then drove herds of cattle from the ranch to New Orleans to sell.

Martín's cattle herd grew to more than 5,000 animals. He also owned many fine horses and mules, which he drove to New Orleans every year to sell.

WILD, WILD HORSES

Horses were first brought to the New World from Spain when the Spanish arrived in the 1500s. Through the years, some horses escaped their Spanish owners or were stolen by Indians. The horses started living off the land and roaming free in areas such as the Texas plains.

*Mustangs still roam free across parts of the United States. They are descended from **domesticated** horses brought to North America by the Spanish.*

FACING WAR

Around 1810, the Spanish government was having problems ruling its people. Many people living in Mexico were unhappy with the Spanish government. People born in Spain were given special rights. Mestizos, or people of Spanish and Indian heritage, and Mexican-born Spaniards were treated unfairly. Some people living in Mexico talked about a civil war. A civil war is a fight between two groups of people living in the same country. People who fight against their own government and try to change it are called **revolutionaries**.

The Battle of Monte de las Cruces in October 1830 was an early victory for Mexico's rebels in their revolt against Spanish rule.

FATHER HIDALGO

A Mexican priest named Miguel Hidalgo y Costilla began the Mexican War of **Independence** on September 16, 1810. He gave a famous speech called "El Grito de Dolores" which, in English, means "The Cry of Dolores." In his speech, he asked the criollos and mestizos to fight against the Spanish for Mexico's independence, or right to rule itself. Father Hidalgo was later captured and killed by Spanish forces in 1811. Others carried on the fight. The war lasted more than 11 years. Mexico gained its independence from Spain on September 27, 1821.

▶ *Father Hidalgo is known as the "father of Mexican independence."*

EFFECTS OF THE WAR

Before 1810, Spanish soldiers were placed at forts called presidios throughout Mexico and Texas to protect settlers, who lived nearby. In 1810, Spain called the soldiers back to protect them from revolutionaries. This meant there was no protection for settlers, such as the De León family, from hostile Indians living nearby. Indian tribes such as the Lipan Apache and the Comanche stole cattle and horses and sometimes killed settlers in their homes.

In 1812, the situation became even more dangerous. Revolutionaries moved to the presidio at La Bahía, near the De León ranch. Soon the Spanish forces came and surrounded the fort. They did not let any supplies get into the fort and the revolutionaries were slowly starving. There was a constant threat that fighting would break out. Martín knew it was not a safe place for his family. They left the ranch and moved back to the Mexican province of Nuevo Santander.

The town of La Bahía grew under the protection of the presidio. In 1829, the name of the town was changed to Goliad in honor of Father Hidalgo. You can spell "Goliad" by rearranging certain letters in "Hidalgo."

4 A NEW COLONY

The De Leóns returned to the Santa Margarita ranch and found it had been ruined while they were gone. Martín and his sons built another ranch on the Aransas River. By 1816, the De León family was once again settled in Texas.

PICKING A LOCATION

Martín continued to sell his cattle, horses, and mules in New Orleans. During one of his trail drives he saw what he believed to be a perfect spot to begin his own colony. The area was near the Guadalupe and Lavaca rivers in Texas.

STEPHEN F. AUSTIN

In 1820 Texas was still a large, open **frontier**. An American named Moses Austin had petitioned the Spanish government to start a colony of American settlers in Texas. At first, Moses was turned down. Later, the government agreed, but they set some rules. To move to Texas, Americans had to become Mexican citizens and practice the **Roman Catholic** faith. Moses died shortly after, but his son Stephen F. Austin carried out his father's plan and became the first Anglo-American empresario in Texas.

▶ *Stephen Austin and Martín De León worked together on a peace treaty with the Karankawa Indians in 1827.*

DUTIES OF AN EMPRESARIO

Empresarios settled and managed groups of colonists in Texas. They gave out land grants to families, and they were in charge of providing protection for the colonists by organizing **militias**. They were also judges and political leaders in the community. Empresarios usually received plots of land as payment for their duties.

Stephen F. Austin was the first Texas empresario. He is shown here distributing land to settlers. Martín performed the same duites in his colony.

MEXICAN INDEPENDENCE

Mexico won the Mexican War of Independence in 1821. The Spanish government was thrown out and a new Mexican government was brought in. The Mexican government wanted Mexican people to settle in Texas so that other countries, such as the United States, did not take over the land. They did not trust the Anglo-American settlers and thought they might try to take the land from the Mexicans.

ANGLO-AMERICAN SETTLEMENTS

By 1823, Stephen Austin had settled nearly 300 American families in southern Texas along the Brazos and Colorado rivers. Martín knew he had to act fast if he was going to get good lands for his sons and daughters to settle and start their own families. He decided to ask the government to start his own colony and become an empresario.

EMPRESARIO

Martín and Patricia's older children were starting to get married and have their own families. Martín had failed to gain support from Spain for starting his own colony, but he decided to try again in Texas, which was under Mexico's control. He thought that if he became empresario for his own colony, he could give land grants to all of his children. As the De León family grew, they could live close by and protect each other.

Martín needed more people than just his family to start a colony. He traveled throughout the Mexican province of Nuevo Santander looking for other Mexicans interested in moving to his colony in Texas. It was difficult to find others interested in moving to Texas because there was still available land in Nuevo Santander. Stories of military and Indian attacks scared would-be settlers. Still, 30 families decided to move to Martín's colony in Texas.

COMANCHE

The Comanche Indians lived in the southern Great Plains area of the United States, in what is now Kansas, Oklahoma, and Texas. They moved to the area in the 1600s. Comanche men were known to be fierce warriors, good hunters, and skilled traders. Comanche women gathered and prepared food.

▶ *The Comanche were nomads, which means they moved from place to place. The Comanche lived in tepees.*

DE LEÓN COLONY

Martín petitioned the Mexican government on April 8, 1824, to start his own colony. The Mexican government gave him the go-ahead just five days later, on April 13, 1824. Martín settled 41 families, including his own married children and their families, on lands between the Guadalupe and Lavaca rivers. With this land grant, Martín De León became the first Mexican empresario to found a colony in Texas.

Each family that Martín brought into his new colony received 4,428 acres (1,792 ha) of land for raising cattle and 177 acres (72 ha) of land for growing crops. Martín also planned to build a nearby town with a main square, a church, and a government office. Colonists could also receive a smaller lot in the newly built town.

The Federal Constitution of the United Mexican States of 1824 divided Mexico into 19 states and 4 federal territories.

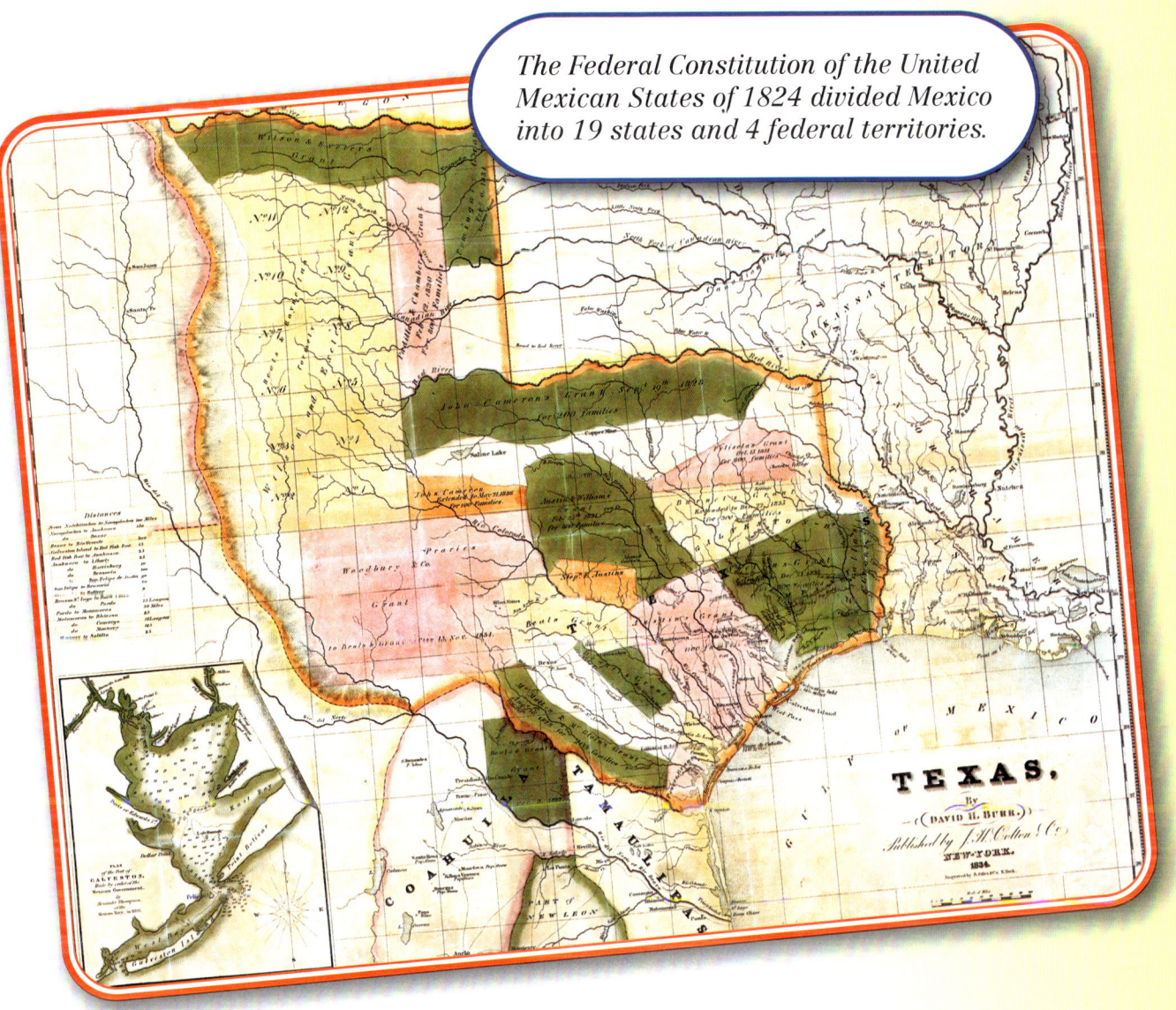

5 VICTORIA

Martín founded his new colony on the Guadalupe River about 30 miles (48 km) away from La Bahía del Espíritu Santo in 1824. He called his new town Villa de Nuestra Señora de Guadalupe de Jesus Victoria. It was a long name, and people shortened it to Victoria. The town was named after a man called Guadalupe Victoria. It was the only colony of Mexican settlers in Texas. There were other colonies in Texas, but the settlers there were all Anglo Americans.

SETTLERS

Although most of the colonists were Mexican, Victoria soon became a multicultural colony that included a few American, Canadian, Irish, French, and German families. Martín's contract for the colony stated that he had to bring in 41 families, but over 100 families ended up moving to Victoria.

From Martín's petition to Governor Juan Arispe, dated May 18, 1827:

" Most Excellent Sir. Citizen Martín De León, Empresario of the Colony of Guadalupe De Jesus de Victoria, in the State of Coahuila and Texas; with due respect represents to your Excellency that ever since the year 1824, he…has endeavored by every means in his power, with great labor and…sacrifices to provide the advancement and prosperity of the settlement, and complete the establishment of the Forty-One families which he proposed at that time… "

Texas Perspective

Martín De León founded the town of Victoria, Texas, for Mexican settlers.

GUADALUPE VICTORIA

Guadalupe Victoria was a soldier and hero who fought for Mexico's independence from Spain in the Mexican war for independence. Victoria became the first elected president of Mexico in 1824 after the country won its independence from Spain. He led the country for almost five years.

The first president of independent Mexico was born with the name Manuel Felix Fernández. He changed it to Guadalupe Victoria during the war.

PATRICIA DE LEON

Martín's wife, Patricia, inherited almost $10,000 from her father. In those days, $10,000 was a lot of money. That amount would be worth over $200,000 today. Patricia believed in her husband's idea to begin a new colony. As an empresario, her husband had to pay to bring the settlers to the colony and establish the town of Victoria. Patricia's money helped with her husband's expenses.

"DON" AND "DOÑA"

After Martín De León became an empresario, he was called Don Martín by the other colonists. His wife was known as Doña Patricia. "Don" and "Doña" are terms that show respect for a person who is a leader in a community.

Martín laid out the town's streets in a Spanish grid plan. The streets were laid out in straight lines and a town block was square-shaped.

LIFE IN THE COLONY

Martín's colony was on a **bluff** that overlooked the Guadalupe River. Large trees such as elm, cypress, live oak, and pecan grew along the riverbank, along with smaller shrubs such as mesquite and huisache. A flat prairie of tall grasses spread away from the river.

Establishing a new town was a lot of work, and Martín was 60 years old when he became an empresario. Martín's four sons, Fernando, Silvestre, Felix, and Agapito, and his son-in-law José Carbajal, helped Martín manage the workload. Don Martín planned the town with José. He marked out where the streets and town lots would be. Fernando helped the new settlers pick out their property for ranches and farms. He became the colony's first land commissioner. Felix and Agapito helped write the government titles and documents.

THE TOWN

According to Mexican law for starting a colony, the new town had to have a church, a town square for trade, a school, and government buildings. Martín and the men used logs cut from the large trees by the riverbank to make buildings. Each family was given a small lot in town and a larger lot outside of the town for a ranch.

WOMEN IN TOWN

The women worked hard to establish the colony, too. Some women prepared meals of tortillas, beans, chilies, and meat for the many hungry workers. In town, the women also put up brush fences, planned gardens, and planted corn, beans, squash, chilies, and tomatoes.

Patricia **donated** $500, which would be worth about $12,000 today, to the Church of Nuestra Señora de Guadalupe to buy furniture and statues. She also established the first school in the town and paid the teacher's salary.

▶ Patricia De León purchased statues of the Virgin of Guadalupe for the colony's church.

THE STREET OF TEN FRIENDS

Martín named the main street of Victoria "Calle de los Diez Amigos," which is Spanish for "The Street of Ten Friends." The ten friends were the people who looked after the colony: Martín; his three sons-in-law: José Carbajal, Placido Benavides, and Rafael Mancholo; his sons, Fernando and Silvestre; two of his children's fathers-in-law, Valentin Garcia and Julian de la Garza; and landowners Leonardo Manso and Pedro Gallardo.

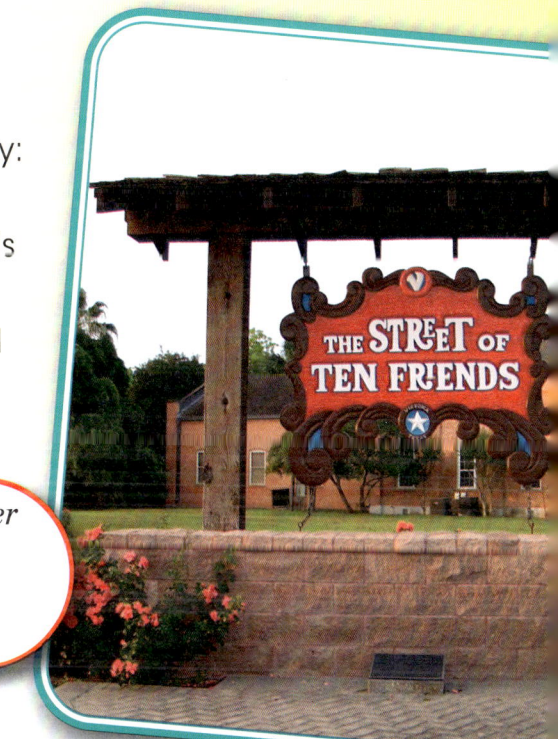

This sign commemorating the former name of Victoria's Main Street is located at the corner of Main and North streets in Victoria, Texas.

25

6 DE LEÓN RANCH

Martín received plots of land as payment for his duties. He received about 30,000 acres (12,141 ha) of land on Garcitas Creek, near the Gulf of Mexico. Martín's land was thought to be the place where the early French explorer Sieur de La Salle first established his colony in the late 1600s. It was close to the Matagorda and Lavaca bays. Martín called his ranch Rancho El Sacramento. It was later called the California Ranch. The ranch is still operating today and is one of the largest cattle ranches in Texas.

After Texas won its independence from Mexico in 1836, the De León family was forced to leave Texas. They abandoned their land, cattle, and most of their possessions. Later attempts to reclaim what had been theirs were not very successful.

CATTLE BRANDING

An animal is branded by burning a mark into its hide, or skin. Cattle have been branded for thousands of years. Each cattle owner had his own brand mark that showed which animals belonged to the ranch. Brands were registered with the government as proof of ownership.

In 1807 Martín became the first rancher in Texas to brand his cattle. Martín's branding mark was an "E" and "J" joined together. The famous brand had been used in the De León family for generations in Spain.

Vaqueros would capture stray cattle and brand them with the De León brand. Martín would then sell them in New Orleans. This helped make Martín very wealthy.

Texas Perspective

Martín De León registered the first cattle brand in Texas.

◀ *The connected "E" and "J" stood for "Espíritus de Jesus," which means the "Spirit of Jesus" in English.*

Vaqueros rounded up cattle at least two times a year, usually in the spring and fall seasons.

ROUNDUP!

Martín's vaqueros rounded up cattle to be branded and sold. The cattle ran in a large group, or herd, of thousands of animals. The vaqueros rode horses to round up the cattle. They then split off some of the cattle into a smaller group to herd into a pen, or fenced-in area.

INDIAN RELATIONS

Martín and the other colonists knew they always had to be on the lookout for Indians such as the Karankawa and Comanche. Although not all Indians were hostile, some would steal cattle and horses and sometimes kill entire families of colonists living in Texas.

By the time he was made empresario of Victoria, Martín knew how to handle Indians who were looking to steal or fight. He would just kill some cows and put on a feast for the Indians! Because of that, some called him "Vacamucha," which means "plenty of cows."

7 LEGACY

More colonists came to Victoria to settle. Martín was pleased with his colony and everything was going well. His ranch was growing to include more horses, cattle, and mules. Martín was a very religious man. He planned to build a new church that would be larger than any other church in Texas or Mexico.

CHOLERA EPIDEMIC OF 1833

During the summer of 1833, a cholera epidemic struck New Orleans and Texas. An epidemic is when many people in an area suffer from a disease. Martín heard that people in Texas were dying of cholera. He thought it was **contagious**, so he told the people living in the town of Victoria to move out to their ranches so they would not catch the disease from others. He also formed a clean-up committee in the town to try to stop the spread of the disease. Sadly, Martín died of the disease in 1833, with his wife and family members by his side. Later, some of the colonists also died from cholera.

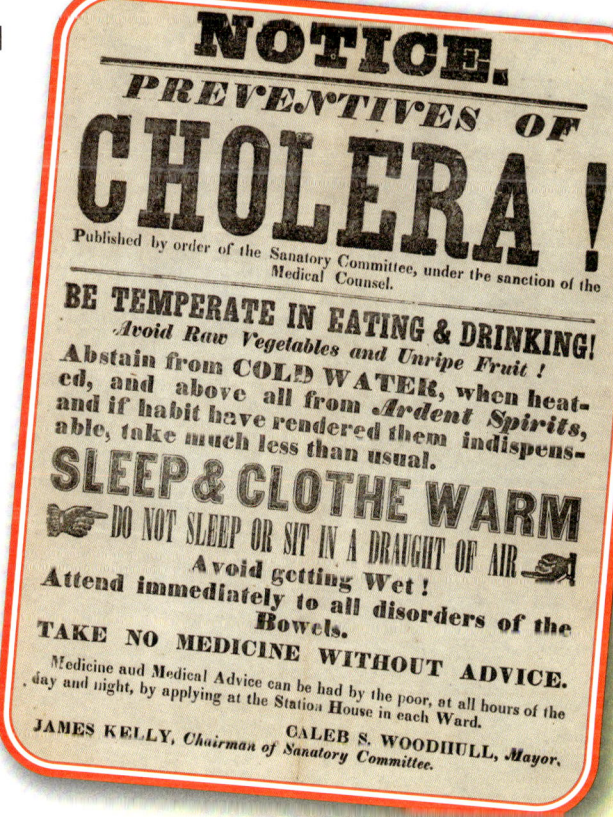

CHOLERA

Cholera is the name of a disease that causes severe diarrhea and vomiting. It is caused by contaminated drinking water, and it is not contagious. Many people in an area get the disease because they drink the same water. Many people got well after having cholera, but more than half the people who had the disease died from severe **dehydration**.

▲ *In the 1800s, the cause of cholera was unknown. There were few doctors and no medicine to treat the disease. Today, antibiotics are used to cure almost all people who have cholera.*

REMEMBERING

During his lifetime, Martín De León was known as a hospitable person who welcomed travelers who needed a place to stay. Martín was a dedicated empresario who cared about his colonists. He was one of the first cattlemen in Texas, and he was also very religious. He was a family man who was loved dearly by his closest family and friends.

> From the historical marker erected in 1936, across the street from Martín's home in Victoria:
>
> " *Martín De León*
> *Born at Burgos, Mexico, 1765. Appointed Captain in the Spanish Army, 1790, for bravery displayed in Indian fighting. Received a grant in 1824 to settle 41 families in Texas. Established the town of Victoria. Received an additional grant in 1829 to settle 150 families. Died in Victoria, 1833. His colony was the only one in which Mexican customs and traditions prevailed.* "

Today, people in Texas are still reminded of Martín. Victoria is now a busy city of more than 60,000 people. The historic downtown features De Leon Plaza, originally called Plaza de la Constitucion by Martin.

LEARNING MORE

BOOKS

Alter, Judy. *Martín de León: Tejano Empresario.* Stars of Texas. Buffalo Gap, TX: State House Press, 2007.

Pickman, Richard. *Anglo-American Colonization of Texas.* New York: Rosen Publishing Group, 2010.

HISTORIC SITES

Presidio La Bahía
www.presidiolabahia.org

WEBSITES

City of Victoria, Texas
www.visitvictoriatexas.com

The De León Colony
www.tamu.edu/faculty/ccbn/dewitt/deleonframe.htm

The Handbook of Texas Online
www.tshaonline.org/handbook

TIMELINE

Texas | **Martín De León**

- **1519** Spain claims New Spain (Mexico) as Spanish colony
- **1682** French explorer Sieur de la Salle claims Louisiana for France
- **1765** Martín De León is born in Burgos, Mexico
- **1785** Martín joins Mexican military
- **1790** Martín joins military regiment of Fieles de Burgos
- **1795** Marries Patricia de la Garza
- **1803** France sells Louisiana to United States
- **1805** Martín De León and his family move and settle in Texas
- **1807** Martín registers first cattle brand used in Texas; asks Mexican government to settle colony but is refused
- **1809** Martín asks to settle colony but is refused
- **September 16, 1810** Mexican War of Independence begins
- **September 27, 1821** Mexico gains independence from Spain
- **December 1821** Stephen F. Austin becomes the first Anglo-American empresario in Texas
- **1823** Drives cattle through Texas to New Orleans, Louisiana
- **1824** Guadalupe Victoria is elected first president of Mexico
- **April 13, 1824** Martín asks to settle colony in Texas and is allowed; becomes empresario and establishes a new colony called Victoria on Guadalupe River in Texas
- **1833** Cholera epidemic strikes Louisiana and Texas
- **1833** Martín dies of cholera
- **April 21, 1836** Texas wins independence from Mexico

GLOSSARY

ancestors (AN-ses-terz) Relatives who lived long ago.
bluff (BLUHF) A high, steep bank or cliff.
Christianity (kris-chee-A-nih-tee) A faith based on the teachings of Jesus Christ and the Bible.
citizens (SIH-tih-zenz) People who were born in or have a right to live in a country or other community.
colony (KAH-luh-nee) A new place where people move that is still ruled by the leaders of the country from which they came.
contagious (kun-TAY-jus) Able to be passed on.
converted (kun-VERT-ed) Changed from one faith to another.
dehydration (dee-hy-DRAY-shun) A condition where the body has lost too much water.
domesticated (duh-MES-tih-kayt-ed) Raised to live with people.
donated (DOH-nayt-ed) Gave something away.
dowry (DOW-ree) The money or property that a woman brings to her husband when they get married.
friar (FRY-ur) A brother in a communal religious order. Friars can be priests.
frontier (frun-TEER) The edge of a settled country, where the wilderness begins.
hospitality (hos-pih-TA-luh-tee) The friendly treatment of guests.
independence (in-dih-PEN-dents) Freedom from the control or support of other people.
militia (muh-LIH-shuh) A group of people who are trained and ready to fight when needed.
nobles (NOH-bulz) People belonging to royalty or having a high rank.
petitioned (puh-TIH-shund) Made a formal written request to ask for something to be done.
promoted (pruh-MOHT-ed) To be raised in rank or importance.
province (PRAH-vins) One of the main parts of a country.
regiment (REH-juh-ment) A group in the military.
revolutionaries (reh-vuh-LOO-shuh-ner-eez) People who fight to change a government.
Roman Catholic (ROH-mun KATH-lik) A Christian religion run by priests and bishops and headed by the pope.
treaty (TREE-tee) An official agreement, signed and agreed upon by each party.

INDEX

Austin, Moses 18
Austin, Stephen 18–20
branding 27–28
Burgos, Mexico 6, 9–10, 30
California Ranch 26
Calle de los Diez Amigos (Street of Ten Friends) 25
cattle 5, 12, 14, 17–18, 21, 26–30
character 5
childhood 6, 8
cholera 29
Christianity 11
civil war 16
Comanche Indians 17, 20, 28
crops 12, 21, 25
De León, Alonso 10
empresario 4–5, 18–24, 28, 30

Father Hidalgo 16–17
Fieles de Burgos 9
France 11
Gallardo, Pedro 25
Garcia, Valentin 25
Garza, Julian de la 25
Garza, Patricia de la 10, 20, 23, 25
Goliad, Texas 17
Guadalupe River 4, 18, 21–22, 24
historical marker 30
jacales 13
Karankawa Indians 18, 28
La Bahía del Espíritu Santo 12–13, 17, 22
land grants 19–21, 30
La Salle, Sieur de 10–11, 26
Lavaca Bay 26
Lavaca River 18, 21

Lipan Apache Indians 17
Louisiana Purchase 11
Manso, Leonardo 25
Matagorda Bay 26
mestizos 9, 16
military career 4, 6, 9, 12
Mission Nuestra Señora de la Purísma Concepción de Acuña 11
muleteers 8
mule trains 4, 8
mustangs 14–15
New Orleans, Louisiana 14, 18, 27, 29
Nuestra Señora de Guadalupe 25
Nuevo Santander 6–9, 17, 20
parents 6

peones 12
petitions 4, 13, 18, 22
presidios 12, 17
Rancho El Sacramento 26
Rancho Santa Margarita 12, 18
revolutionaries 16–17
Roman Catholicism 5, 18
San Antonio River 11–12
vaqueros 12, 14, 27–28
Victoria, Guadalupe 22–23
Victoria (town) 22–25, 28–30

32

B L579P CEN
Peppas, Lynn.
Why Mart+¡n de L+¬on matters to Texas /
CENTRAL LIBRARY
12/14

Friends of the
Houston Public Library